Friends

One Hundred Quotes and Thoughts
With One Hundred Paintings of Lord Ganesha

R.N. Kogata ● **Lalita Kogata**

D.K. Printworld (P) Ltd.
New Delhi

First published in India, 2012
ISBN 13: 978-81-246-0620-9
ISBN 10: 81-246-0620-X

© Paintings: Mahadev Exports
© Text: R N Kogata & Lalita Kogata

All rights reserved. No part of this publication, text and photographs, may be reproduced or transmitted, except brief quotations, in any form or by any means, electronic or mechanical, including photocopying, recording, or any information storage or retrieval system, without prior written permission of the copyright holder, indicated above, and the publishers.

A creation of:
Mr R N Kogata & Mrs Lalita Kogata
608, Hiran Magari, Sector-11, Udaipur - India
Phone : +91-94141-58870, +91-294-2583870
e-mail: devkush@rediffmail.com

Published and printed by:
D.K. Printworld (P) Ltd.
"Vedaśrī" F-395, Sudarshan Park
(Metro Station: Ramesh Nagar), New Delhi - 110 015
Phs.: 011-2545 3975, 2546 6019
Fax: 011-2546 5926
e-mail: indology@dkprintworld.com
Web: www.dkprintworld.com

Preface

It is said and we all know that a friend is a person who feels your feelings, comes in your life when the whole world walks out, he brightens your life, he believes in you and is always ready to be with you under all circumstances, positive or negative, happy or sad, good or bad.

We can define the friend as 'F – Field of love', 'R – Root of joy', 'I – Island of God', 'E – End of sorrow', 'N – Name of hope' and 'D – Door of understanding'.

Everyone knows many things about friends and friendship but usually no one practises them in practical life. We have always felt that if something is put forth in a systematic manner before anybody, he will immediately understand the meaning of the same as also realise the importance of it. We have, therefore, tried to put together and present some inspiring quotes, thoughts and sayings on friends and friendship. We believe that these expressions and representations, covering various facets of true friendship, will illuminate many more minds with love and care for unification of mankind, where more and more people become friends . . . with no place for enmity and enemies; friends become good friends and good friends become the best friends and the world comprises only friends and no enemies.

We are sure that these incisive and insightful quotes, thoughts and ideas selected and presented in a unique way, with matching illustrations of the Lord Ganesha, in this book, would open up new dimensions of friendship amongst the friends and that you would pass them on to others in order to inspire them to become even better individuals and the best of friends. The paintings alongside quotes, have been created by our professional artists keeping in mind the theme of each individual quote.

Some of the thoughts presented here are ours and others are from the people who have stood by and worked for the values; some were famous names and some others were ordinary people. We have tried to indicate in the acknowledgement page, names of the persons whose quote we have reproduced wherever we could remember. Any amendment/addition in this regard is most welcome from the learned readers.

Our sincere thanks to Barbara De Angelis, William Arthur Ward, Anais Nin, Samuel Johnson, Shawn Swain, Jeremy Taylor, Thomas Wilson, James Fenimore Cooper, Stephen Ambrose, G.T. HewittIf, Emerson, Ralph Waldo, Charles Caleb Colton, G. Randolf, Epicurus, Joseph Mercier, Axel Munthe, Stephanie, who have given such invaluable thoughts to this world.

We prostrate before our parents Smt Kanchan Devi and Shri Bhairav Lal Kogata, and Smt Kamla Devi Nuwal and the late Prof K.M. Nuwal for their benign blessings that have guided us throughout and made us reach the stage where we find ourselves today.

With the expectation of blessings and constructive feedback from all of you.

Lalita & R.N. Kogata

Acknowledgements

Quotations of the following great personalities have been included in this book:

Quote appeared on page no.	By
9	Barbara De Angelis
23	William Arthur Ward
31	Anais Nin
41	Samuel Johnson
46	Shawn Swain
49	Jeremy Taylor
51	Thomas Wilson
53	James Fenimore Cooper
56	Stephen Ambrose
81	G.T. Hewittif

86	Emerson Ralph Waldo
93	Charles Caleb Colton
94	G. Randolf
96	Epicurus
97	Desire-Joseph Mercier
99	Axel Munthe
104	Strephanie

A best friend is one
who just comes in
when the whole world is out.

A friend comes to party
and offers a gift.

But a real friend stays back
after the party
and helps you
to clean the home.

A friend is like a rainbow.

He brightens your life
when you have been through a storm.

A friend
is one of the nicest things
you can have,

and

one of the best things
you can be.

A friend is one
who believes in you,

when you have ceased
to believe in yourself.

A friend will joyfully sing with you when you are on the mountain top

and silently walk beside you through the dark, deep valley.

A good friend is like a computer;

'enter' into your life,

'save' you in his heart,

'format' your problems,

'shift' you to opportunities

and never 'delete' you from memory.

A friendship founded on business

is better than

a business founded on friendship.

A friend will always see
you through
after others see
you are through.

A good friend is one, who can tell you all his problems but doesn't.

A man never gets so rich
that he can ever afford
to lose a friend.

A real friend
never gets in your way
unless you happen to be
on the way down.

A ring is round
and has no ends.

That is how long
we will remain friends.

A true friend is not like
a shower of rain
that pours and goes.

It is more like air, though
sometimes keeping quiet
but is always there;
constantly hanging around.

A true friend is someone
who knows that
there is something wrong
even when you have
the biggest smile on your face.

A true friend is someone who reaches for your hand but touches your heart.

A true friend knows your weaknesses
   but shows you your strengths;

feels your fears but fortifies your faith;

sees your anxieties but frees your spirit;

recognises your inabilities
   but emphasises your possibilities.

A valuable friend is one,
who will tell you
what you should be told,
even if it momentarily offends you.

Anybody can say
'I understand your feelings'.

But a real friend says
'I feel your feelings'.

Be ever cautious to choose your friends

and

be even more cautious
in changing them.

Beware of friends like your own shadow,
you see them only when the sun shines.

Don't love your best friend like a flower,
because flower dies after a season.

Love your best friend like a river,
because it flows forever without any reason.

Don't walk in front of me,
I may not follow.

Don't walk behind me,
I may not lead.

Just walk beside me
and be my friend.

During our friendship,
there will be times . . .
you would not see me beside you.

Don't think I left you behind,

I just chose to walk behind you
so I can catch you when you fall.

Each friend represents a world in us,
a world possibly not born until they arrive,
and it is only by this meeting
that a new world is born.

Every memory of friendship shared,
even for a short time, is a treasure,

like sunshine and warmth in our lives,

like a cool breeze on a humid day,

like a shower of rain refreshing the earth.

F — Field of love.
R — Root of joy.
I — Island of God.
E — End of sorrow.
N — Name of hope.
D — Door of understanding.

That is FRIEND.

True friends are like diamonds...

They shine more when it is dark!

Friends are like stars;

you can't always see them,
but you know
they are always there for you!

Friendship —
- F – Fun, Faith
- R – Rational, Righteousness
- I – Impartial, Integrity
- E – Emotional, Elegance
- N – Never Ending, Nobility
- D – Dependable, Dedication
- S – Special, Sincerity
- H – Heart Warming, Humanity
- I – Interesting, Intimacy
- P – Priceless, Perseverance

Friendship gives two people
something or the other
to share, like a happy evening
filled with fun and laughter,
or even a quiet comfortable day.

Friendship is a bond,
a relationship, and a feeling,

take it anyway,
it leaves the heart
with a warm sensation.

Friendship is a magic weaver.

It brings happiness
to the heart
and adds magic
to everything around.

Friendship is a promise made in the heart . . . silently . . . unwritten . . . unbreakable by distance . . . unchangeable by time . . . unforgettable by mind . . .

Friendship is a union of spirits,
a marriage of hearts,
and the bond of virtue.

Friendship is like a bank account,
in which you have to deposit
love, sympathy, trust, and joy . . .

and as interest you will get
True companion for a lifetime.

Friendship is like a garden.

It is beautiful when watered with love, care, affections, tears, cheers.

But it dries up if left untouched;

So keep in touch.

Friendship is like a tree . . .
it is not measured as how tall it could be,
but how deep the roots have grown.

Friendship is not how you forget
but how you forgive,

Not how you listen
but how you understand,

Not what you see
but how you feel, and

Not how you let go
but how you hold on.

Friendship is precious,
not only in the shade,
but also in the sunshine of life;

and thanks to a benevolent arrangement of things,
the greater part of life is sunshine.

Friendship is like a sheltering tree.

It is a warm shade of love and care,
always willing to protect and prevent.

Friendship is a silent gift of nature —

More old more strong,

More deep more clear,

More close more warm,

Less words more understanding.

Friendship is the allay of our sorrows,
the ease of our passions,
the discharge of our oppressions,
the sanctuary to our calamities,
the counsellor of our doubts,
and the clarity of our minds.

Friendship is the shadow
of the evening,
which strengthens
with the setting sun of life.

Friendship is to be purchased
only by friendship.

A man may have authority over others,
but he can never have their hearts
but by giving his own.

Friendship is wanting to share with one another,

it is wanting to care for one another;

it is the promise of lasting commitment.

Friendship that flows from the heart cannot be frozen by adversity,

as the water that flows from the spring cannot congeal in winter.

Friendship will last

if it is put first.

Friendship,
with time becomes deeper and matured
and weaves a colourful tapestry of memories,
of moments spent in the company of friends.

Friendship is different
 from all other relationships.
Unlike acquaintanceship,
 friendship is based on love.
Unlike lovers and married couples,
 it is free of jealousy.
Unlike children and parents,
 it knows neither criticism nor resentment.
Friendship has no status in law.
Business partnerships are based
 on a contract;
So is marriage,
Parents are bound by law.
But friendship is freely entered into,
 freely given, and freely exercised.

God is so wise
that he never created friends
with price tags,

Because . . .
if he did,
I wouldn't afford
a precious friend like you.

Good friends are those —

who care without hesitation,

who tolerate without frustration,

who remember without limitation, and

who love even without communication.

He is the kind of a friend

who will always be there . . .

when he needs you!

I asked God for a flower,
he gave me a garden.

I asked for a tree,
he gave me a forest.

I asked for a river,
he gave me an ocean.

I asked for a friend,
he gave me YOU.

I don't remember
how we happened to meet each other.

I don't even remember
who got along with whom first.

All I can remember is
both of us are together,
always . . .

If all my friends
were to jump off a building,

I would not jump with them;

I would be on the ground
to catch them.

If friends were flowers
I would not pick them.

I would let them grow in the garden,
and cultivate them with love and care
so I could keep them as friends forever.

If I could pull down the rainbow
I would write your name with it
and put it back in the sky
to let everybody know
how colourful my life is
with a friend like you.

In the end,
we will remember
not the words of our enemies
but the "silence" of our friends.

It is better
to keep a friend from falling
than to help him stand up
after he falls.

It is true that we don't know
what we have got until we lose it,
but it's also true
that we don't know
what we have been missing
until it arrives.

It takes half our life
to find true friends
and half of it
keeping them.

I am lucky to have spent
less than half of my life
finding a friend
and wish to spend the rest
keeping him.

Many people will walk
in and out
of your life,

but only true friends
will leave footprints
in your heart.

My friend,
I like one thing about you...

That you are very sentimental...

just 1% senti

but 99% mental!!!

Never say you are happy,
when you are somewhat sad.

Never say you are fine,
when you are not in best of spirits.

Never say you feel good,
when you feel a little bit bad.

And Never say you are alone,
when I am still alive and along!

No lapse of time or distance of place can lessen the friendship of those who are truly persuaded of each other's worth.

No matter
how strong a friendship may be,

it takes years to build the trust,
and seconds to destroy it.

Our friendship is a blank cheque for me.

It's an ASSET not a LIABILITY.

Always a CREDIT not DEBIT.

Always a PROFIT not a LOSS.

And I know it will never bounce.

Our friendship means so much to me

that if we were the last people on a sinking ship

and we had only one life jacket …

I would hmmm …

I will miss you …

Promises may get friends
but it is performance
that keeps them.

Real Friend —

- Tells you when your face is dirty.

- Can be called at 4:00 a.m., which matters.

- Stands for you in adversity.

- Walks in when the rest of world walks out.

Some friends are worth to be thrown,..
some are good to keep,
some are to be treasured forever, and

I think you are the one to be thrown
into the treasure box to be kept forever.

Some people may still have their first dollar

but the man who is really wealthy is the fellow who still has his first friend.

Someone asked me
for how long will we both be friends.

I remained silent because
I did not know which one is longer
"ALWAYS" or "FOREVER".

The best things in life are never rationed.

Friendship, loyalty and love do not require coupons.

The best way to destroy an enemy is to make him a friend.

The difference between our friends and enemies is –

Our friends love us in spite of our faults

and our enemies hate us in spite of our virtues.

The friend

who can be silent with us
in a moment of despair or confusion,

who can stay with us
in the hour of grief and bereavement,

who can tolerate not knowing, not curing, not healing
and face with us the reality of our powerlessness —

that is the friend who really cares.

The gift of friendship is that
it takes us by the hand
and reminds us,
we are not alone
in the journey of life.

The glory of friendship is not the outstretched hand, nor the kindly smile nor the joy of companionship;

it is the spiritual inspiration that comes to one when he discovers that someone else believes in him and is willing to trust him.

The more arguments you win,

the fewer friends you will have.

The value of a friend cannot be measured...

Only treasured.

There is an important difference between love and friendship.

While the former delights in extremes and opposites, the latter demands equality.

There is only one reason
why your enemy
can't become your friend –

YOU!

True friends are like diamonds...
They are real and rare.

False friends are like leaves...
They are scattered everywhere.

True friends are like mornings,
you can't have them the whole day,
but you can be sure,
they will be there when you wake up
tomorrow, next year and forever.

True friendship is like sound health;

the value of it is seldom known until it is lost.

Truly great friends

are hard to find,

difficult to leave

and impossible to forget.

We are on the wrong track
when we think of friendship
as something to get

rather than
something to give.

We do not so much need
the help of our friends
as the confidence of
their help in need.

We must not only give
what we have;

we must also give
what we are.

What is a Friend?

A friend is someone
you can depend on.

Someone who you can talk to,

who knows all about you
and still likes you,

who is there with you
through all thick and thin.

What you keep to yourself
you lose,

what you give away,
you keep forever.

When a friend makes a mistake,

don't rub it in.

Rub it out!

When a man
borrows money from a bank
he pays interest;

but when he borrows
from a friend
he often loses interest.

When friendship is deeply rooted,

it is like a plant
that cannot even be
uprooted by a storm.

When I am walking in front of you,
I am protecting you.

When I am beside you,
I am there for you.

When I am behind you,
I am watching over you.

When I am alone,
I am thinking of you.

Within you
I lose myself,

without you
I find myself
wanting to be lost again.

You are alive.

Do something –

Look, Listen, Choose, Act

and Make Friends.

You cannot say you've lost a friend.

If a friendship is capable of ending, it is because it never existed.